A souvenir guide

Brockhampton Estate
Herefordshire

Amy Feldman

G000044517

National Trust

The Heart of Herefordshire

With its gentle, picturesque moat, endearingly slanted Gatehouse and charming timber-framing, Lower Brockhampton Manor is 'everything an English manor house should be' (Tom Quinn, Hidden Britain, 2005).

Once inside, the Manor takes you on a journey through its history, each room uncovering a person or family who lived and worked here from the 15th century right up to the last tenants in the 1950s. It reveals an heiress with a very specific bedtime routine, a 13-year-old millionaire and philanthropist, a young First World War volunteer, 20th-century farmers and many more.

Yet if it hadn't been for the serendipitous visit of architect John Buckler in 1871, Lower Brockhampton might have crumbled into ruin. Brockhampton's owners decamped from the Manor in the 1700s, after creating a more fashionable mansion on higher ground. Lower Brockhampton was used as a farmhouse and soon became dilapidated. But after Buckler recognised its historical significance, it became the subject of an extensive, ambitious restoration project (see page 10).

While Lower Brockhampton is arguably the estate's emblem, there is much more to these 690 hectares (1,700 acres). Designed naturalistic parkland meshes with ancient woods. Farmers work the fields and productive orchards, continuing a tradition that dates back hundreds, possibly even thousands, of years.

Whether you would like to take a stroll through unspoilt historical woods, discover five centuries of history or relax with a picnic overlooking the Herefordshire countryside, Brockhampton will delight and inspire you.

'Everyone who thinks of England as a country full of quaint thatched cottages and "ye olde oake" timber-framed buildings must catch their breath when they first set eyes on Lower Brockhampton manor'

– Christopher Simon Sykes, *Ancient English Houses*, 1988

Location, location, location

Fifteenth-century Lower Brockhampton Manor's location in the hollow of a damson orchard reveals something about what was valued by its first inhabitants. Three hundred years later, the estate's owners built a new house high on the hills to take advantage of the expansive views. But in the medieval period, easy access to water was a key concern, which is why the first manor was built lower down.

Top A view across the Brockhampton Estate in autumn, looking towards the Abberley Hills and beyond

Bottom A view of Lower Brockhampton Manor's Gatehouse, with the Manor itself beyond

A Brief History

Brockhampton has been occupied in one way or another since the 12th century.

The name, Brockhampton, indicates that there was a settlement here in Anglo Saxon times but the first official mention appears in the 12th century, when a knight rented a hide of land (50 hectares, or 120 acres) from the Bishop of Hereford. By 1166, the knight is referred to as Bernard of Brockhampton, the earliest record of the estate's name. We know very little else about Bernard and his household – the first known occupation of Brockhampton comes after their time but they were likely responsible for building the first chapel here (see page 32).

We know even less about their successor, Robert de Furches, to whom the Brockhamptons sold land from the estate in 1283. Despite being the first family recorded as living here, neither he, nor any other Brockhampton resident of the following century, can be traced on the estate today.

The same certainly isn't true of the Brockhamptons' successors, the Domultons (also referred to as the Dumbletons). In the late 14th century, John Domulton – who came from Dumbleton in Gloucestershire to marry Emma Brockhampton – renovated the Chapel. It was for him that Lower Brockhampton Manor was built, the Great Hall and east wing completed in c.1425.

Brockhampton was later passed to John and Emma's son Philip. After Philip, Brockhampton passed to his son, another John, who married Agnes Croft of nearby Croft Castle (now also National Trust), and then to John's daughter Elizabeth.

The Habingtons

Early in the 15th century, Elizabeth Domulton married William Habington. Their grandson, Richard Habington the 2nd (died 1545), made significant changes to Lower Brockhampton from around 1520–8, including building the kitchen wing and rebuilding part of the east block. Richard was also responsible for some of the Manor's more ostentatious additions: the close studding (extra timbers) in the south and east walls, and the Gatehouse, both Tudor status symbols.

Left Lower Brockhampton Manor from behind. Here you can see examples of expensive close studding (see page 24) and, behind the tree, the chimney (see page 16)

Right Volunteer Terry Jamieson in character as Philip Domulton

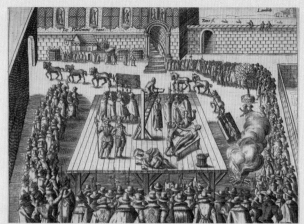

What's in a name?

Richard Habington's younger brother John (1515–1581) worked for four monarchs and was cofferer to Queen Elizabeth I. The Cofferer of the Household was the highest position on the board of Green Cloth, a group of senior officials who looked after the practical aspects of life at court. The Cofferer was responsible for most of the money that passed through the Household and was also head of the Counting House.

Yet John's life might have taken a very different turn: in 1529, he was accused of murder.

The accuser was a William Housseman who claimed that, seven years earlier, the young boy John shot an arrow that killed William's brother, Roger, 'wilfully and with malicious intent'. In defence, John claimed that Roger fell on his own arrow, a story supported by friends who had been with him at the time of the accident. John was never convicted, enabling him to pursue his career at court.

One of John's sons, Edward, continued the family's bloody tradition. In 1586, he was convicted for his involvement in the Babington plot, which planned to free the imprisoned Mary, Queen of Scots and assassinate Queen Elizabeth I. Edward, along with the plot's leaders, was hung, then drawn and quartered – a particularly barbaric process.

Edward's brother, Thomas – whose godmother was Queen Elizabeth I – survived being found guilty of both the Babington and Gunpowder plots. He lived to be 87.

Richard and his wife Joyce Shirley had three daughters, Mary, Eleanor and Jane. In 1552, Mary's marriage to Richard Barneby brought the longest-standing Brockhampton family to the estate.

The Barnebys/Lutleys

Richard and Mary's descendants lived here for almost four hundred years, but they were not always called Barneby. When John Barneby left the estate to his nephew Bartholomew Lutley in 1726, he demanded that he change his name to Barneby. In 1865 John Habington Barneby changed his name back to Lutley after a family dispute.

In their early days of ownership, the family made a number of changes to the house. Then in the 1700s, Bartholomew Barneby had a new Georgian mansion built at the top of the estate. Lower Brockhampton Manor was converted into a farmhouse, and was never again inhabited by a member of the Barneby family.

Bartholomew still took good care of Lower Brockhampton, but his descendants spent less time and money on the Manor and so it began to wither away. That was until 1870, when the renowned architect JC Buckler undertook a huge restoration project (see page 10).

The last of the family was John Talbot Lutley, who left the estate to the National Trust.

'[a] tall, ungainly, pipe-smoking countryman'
– James Lees-Milne, *People and Places*, 1992

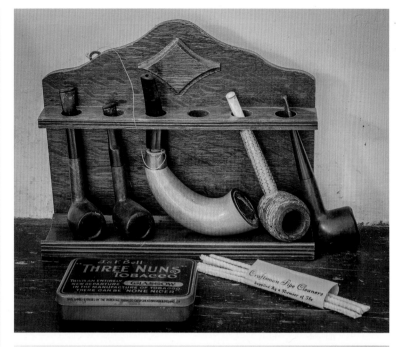

Colonel Lutley and his bequest

Colonel John Talbot Lutley (1873–1946) was the 17th generation of the family to live at Brockhampton. He would also be the last. In his will, Colonel Lutley bequeathed the entire estate to the National Trust.

Lutley took over Brockhampton in 1906, having inherited the estate on his father's death. At the time, Lower Brockhampton Manor remained a farmhouse; Lutley always lived in Bartholomew's mansion.

Lutley was first and foremost a military man and was a veteran of the Boer War of 1899–1902. His last role in the army was training volunteers for service with the Worcestershire Yeomanry during the First World War, after which he retired. He went on to serve as a Justice of the Peace. He also spent a lot of time taking care of his cherished estate, and he was particularly proud of his trees. He was careful to stay clean while doing his rounds, though, keeping fresh boots at many of the estate cottages, which he changed into if the pair he was wearing got muddy.

After visiting Brockhampton in 1938, James Lees-Milne (secretary of the National Trust's Country House Committee) described the older Colonel Lutley as the perfect example of an early 20th-century bachelor: 'shy, remote and almost irreproachably polite'. Lutley's housekeeper, Mrs Hughes, and butler, Bakewell, remembered him affectionately, as 'a disciplinarian of the old school, but God-fearing and just'. (James Lees-Milne, *People and Places*, 1992)

The Colonel's final years were marred by crippling arthritis. The former army veteran solider became reliant upon Bakewell to care for him, a round-the-clock job for which the butler earned £2 a week. Without Lutley to look after it, Brockhampton mirrored its master's decline.

Left Colonel John Talbot Lutley's belongings at Brockhampton today

Centre A pencil and watercolour illustration of Colonel John Talbot Lutley in uniform, dating from 1915.

The artist, Brian Hatton, was killed in action in 1916

Top right A collection of pipes on display at Brockhampton

Bottom right A view to Bartholomew's mansion, in which Colonel Lutley lived (now leased privately)

The Trust comes to Brockhampton

Colonel Lutley had no descendants. His heirs were two cousins, but Lutley's father, John, had fallen out with their families in 1865. We don't know what the disagreement was about, but it prompted John to disassociate himself from them by changing his surname from Barneby to Lutley.

It is perhaps this lack of a suitable heir that, in 1938, prompted Colonel Lutley to write to the National Trust enquiring if they would be interested in his Midlands estate. The answer must have been yes, because on Lutley's death in 1946, the entire 690-hectare (1700-acre) estate, complete with two large houses, four farms and a number of smaller cottages, was bequeathed to the National Trust, ending 573 years of family ownership. In his will, Lutley asked that Lower Brockhampton be 'appropriately furnished and shown to the public', which it has been in some form ever since. However he left no instructions for the Georgian mansion, which the Trust decided wasn't architecturally significant enough to open to the public. So, with a view to privately letting the house, its contents were removed. Some were used to furnish other recently-acquired properties, such as Montacute House in Somerset. Others were sold at auction in Worcester. Only a handful were kept and moved to Lower Brockhampton, such as the dining tables, Lutley's gun collection and family portraits now in the Great Hall, and some leather fire buckets.

'Lunched in the cold, cold hall and walked around the house
where Colonel Lutley's personal belongings are left lying
about since the day he died. Something poignant in a house
which has suddenly ceased to exist with the last owner. Life
arrested in old tobacco jars with the lids off, smelly old pipes,
books turned face downwards on tables, the well-worn
favourite chair with deep imprint of the late "behind" and
threadbare arms, and the mournful, reproachful gaze of
dozens of forgotten ancestors on the walls.'

– James Lees-Milne describes a visit to the Georgian house following
Colonel Lutley's death in 1946, *People and Places*, 1992

Saving Brockhampton: Buckler's restoration

'The preservation of Brockhampton old House has been a labour of love'

– John Buckler, 1871

In 1871, Lower Brockhampton was no longer the main seat of the Barneby family, who had long since moved to the Georgian mansion at the head of the estate. Lower Brockhampton was being used as a farmhouse, and slowly falling into disrepair. If it hadn't been for John Buckler it may not have survived.

When he arrived at Brockhampton, Buckler (1793–1894) was already a well-known architect. He had officially retired from an illustrious career that included careful restorations of Lincoln Cathedral, Oxburgh Hall in Norfolk (now also National Trust) and Oxford University's Magdalen and Jesus colleges. He also frequently contributed to *Gentleman's Magazine* as an 'Architectural Antiquary' and came second in a competition to design the new Houses of Parliament after the original was destroyed by fire in 1834.

When Buckler discovered Lower Brockhampton, it was over 100 years since the family had left the manor house. That's not to say the family intentionally let Lower Brockhampton deteriorate. Buckler himself wrote that 'regard for the home of many and ancient generations has never been exhausted … it has at no time been violently injured or carelessly neglected'. It simply suffered from being an old timber-framed house, with no resident wealthy landlord to make necessary improvements.

Many believed restoring the Manor was a hopeless task. But not the estate's then-owner, John Habington Lutley (John Talbot Lutley's father), who agreed to Buckler's plans. And so, working with Oxford builder John Fisher, Buckler embarked on his ambitious restoration.

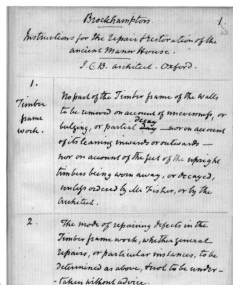

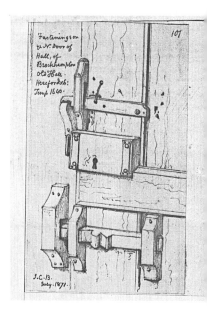

Left An oil painting of John Buckler, painted by William Riviere, in Oxford, 1872

Above left A diamond pane window on the ground floor of Brockhampton (windows like this were installed in Buckler's time but the one in situ now dates from the 1950s)

Above centre An extract from Buckler's notebook on the Brockhampton restoration

Above right Buckler's illustration of a door latch for Brockhampton, dated 1871

The repairs

Buckler was adamant that his renovation should not be 'derogatory to the antiquity' of the Manor: crooked limbs were not straightened, irregular lines of walls 'pardoned'. He left strict instructions to those working on the Manor, stating repairs to material should only be made if absolutely essential. If new materials had to be used then they were treated to look like the old: timbers were stained, bricks lime-whitened. Any deviations from the instructions could only be authorised by himself or Fisher. In 1978, Julian Munby described the work as 'an outstanding example of sympathetic conservation that could scarcely be paralleled today' (*Oxoniensia* journal, 1978).

Where did the work take place?

Most repairs were undertaken in the Great Hall (see page 18). Here Buckler removed a bedroom floor and three dormer windows in the roof, all of which had been inserted for John Barneby in the mid-17th century. The floor was repaved using flagstones from elsewhere in the manor house. He also designed and inserted the staircase that now leads to the Gallery, and new windows replacing casements cut into the timber frame at an earlier date (these have since been replaced by copies made in 1950). Elsewhere, the wall of the kitchen was restored and the floor paved with bricks laid flat. Brickwork throughout the building was conserved and repointed if possible or replaced if too severely damaged, and the roof tiling was repaired. Brockhampton was once again the perfect example of a quaint medieval, timber-framed abode.

Exploring Lower Brockhampton Manor

The Moat

This would once have provided the household with food such as fish, water plants and the occasional duck. However its main role was to impress: it is too small to have been a serious defensive feature, and moats were a well-known status symbol in medieval England. They 'gave to the site the character required by custom, established by rank and sanctioned by antiquity' (John Buckler, 1871).

Today the moat is a peaceful haven for ducks, moorhens and pied and grey wagtails, as well as damselflies, dragonflies and pond skaters.

Constructing the moat

This feature presents two mysteries: was it ever a complete circle? And when was it built?

The first question remains unanswered. However for the second we can make some assumptions: pottery evidence dating from between the 15th and 16th centuries was found in the cut of land later filled by debris from the moat. So the moat was probably dug for the Domultons around the same time, or perhaps just after, the Manor was first built. However the Gatehouse that crosses it dates from 100 years later, built for the Habingtons (see page 14) – could the moat have been constructed at the same time?

The moat also once had an overflow channel: built at the same time as the moat, this was a stone-lined drain that controlled overflow from the moat and directed it to a natural spring line to the south east. By 1829 a sluice linked the moat to a new rectangular pond. This made the overflow channel redundant, but it found a new purpose in demarking an area of gardens along the moat's northern edge.

Left The front of the Manor seen across the moat from the south east

Above right The stunning view from the south side of the moat

Some other features

Sometime between the estate surveys of 1737 and 1829, two more water features were constructed: a pond to the south east of the moat and Manor, and, to the east, a small pond which surrounded a rectangular island. Too small to have supported a structure of any consequence, the island was probably used by the Barneby family to safeguard wild fowl.

The Gatehouse

Wolves and bandits no longer prowled these Herefordshire hills when the Gatehouse was built for the Habingtons in 1543; so it's unlikely this two-storeyed, delightfully lopsided building was constructed for defensive purposes. Instead it, like the moat, was a form of wealth display, alerting guests that they were visiting an important family. It has also been described a visual pun, an aesthetically pleasing miniature of the Manor behind.

Inside, look out for double Vs on the walls. These religious marks symbolise the Virgin Mary. As Protestants don't pray to Mary, these inscriptions support rumours that then-illegal Catholic masses were once held here (with the exception of three years under James II (1685–8), England was a strictly Protestant country from 1559 to 1791).

Today, as well as providing a grand entrance to Lower Brockhampton, the Gatehouse is used by swallows and house martins as a nesting spot in the summer months.

The details

The Gatehouse has been updated and repaired significantly since it was built. The staircase is a 17th-century addition, replacing a ladder; the grapevine-carved bargeboards on the south gables are modern copies of decayed Tudor ones; and the whole building underwent major restoration work in 1999. However, the 'quite perfect' studded door (Buckler, 1871) and bargeboards at the back (north) entrance are original to the building.

Burn marks

If you look closely at the Gatehouse's far wall and staircase corridor, you might notice some dark marks that look like imperfections in the wood. These are in fact 'burn marks', commonly found on the inside of 15th- to 18th-century timber-framed buildings across northern Europe. Once thought to be careless accidents, it's now believed there's much more to these mysterious marks, which were probably scorched onto timber using special types of candles and could have taken up to fifteen minutes to produce.

These superstitious marks were intended to protect the building from fire damage.

Left The wonky Gatehouse perched over the moat

Top right A view to the Manor from underneath the Gatehouse

Bottom right The top floor of the Gatehouse

The Parlour
The Screens Passage

The Parlour

With its printed hanging weaving together the lives of the families who lived and worked at Brockhampton, the Parlour is the ideal spot to get your bearings about the Manor and its history.

Originally this room was a pantry for storing dry food. We think it was modernised to become a Parlour in c.1610, when a number of alterations were made to the house for John Barneby.

The panelling

Installed in the early 17th century, the panelling on the north wall presents something of a mystery. We know it wasn't made for this room, as it doesn't fit properly – the panelling is incomplete and there is a redundant door on the side closest to the printed hanging. Yet the Habingtons, for whom it was installed, were extremely wealthy and had no need to buy second-hand furnishings. One theory is that it was rescued from a religious building or other treasured relic which may have been under threat of demolition during the Reformation.

The bricks

Take a look at the bricks at the base of the Parlour's outside wall, by the chimney. These are the oldest in Brockhampton, and have been in this position since the medieval era.

Most bricks used in the Manor and granary were machine-made in the Victorian period or later. However these particular ones are much smaller than the others, by about 12mm all over.

They also appear to have been dried in the open air and fired in a simple kiln. Their shape identifies them as being the product of master tiler and travelling brickmaker John Byrd, who was in this area between 1420 and 1430 – the same time that John Domulton was building his new manor house.

John Byrd's bricks can also be seen in two panels between the drainpipe and window, where they were moved when the chimney was rebuilt by Buckler in 1870.

Top left A fire-surround in the Parlour

Bottom left The Parlour's spinning wheel

Top right A view of the Parlour

The ceiling

Only some of the ceiling here – by the panelling – is original. Elsewhere it appears a new, thin layer of plaster has been applied. Could this have been a necessity following a minor domestic disaster in the room above, such as a flood that came through the ceiling?

The artefacts

On the west wall are a beautiful calligraphy birthday card received by John Talbot Lutley, and a welcome home card given when he returned from his first military posting in South Africa. The elaborate detailing on both gives an idea of quite how respected the Colonel – and the family in general – was in the local community.

The Screens Passage

Screens passages were common in manor houses like Brockhampton, marking the entrance to the Great Hall. They also helped keep out draughts and mask servants' activities in the store rooms. Brockhampton's Screens Passage was originally marked by movable screens; the permanent wall was modified in 1870, during Buckler's restoration project.

The Great Hall

The Great Hall was the most important space in a medieval home, and in the Domultons' day this room – which was as wide and high as money could buy – would have been a constant hub of activity. Most key activities took place here, from sleeping, eating and socialising to training dogs and hiring servants.

A quality construct

Like the Moat and Gatehouse, the Great Hall was an opportunity to make an impression. The wooden frame was expensive to build, as the tall crucks (long, curved timbers) had to be cut from very large trees with just the right curve in their trunk. The collar beam that joins them at the top allowed the Hall extra width. The crucks are moulded, with battlements carved at the angle. The rest of the carpentry is also of a high quality: the struts supporting the roof apex form quatrefoil (four-lobed) openings. The windbraces, which steady the roof against gales, have been cusped to match them.

A new use

By the time the first John Barneby was living here in the early 17th century, 'the medieval hall was dead' (Gomme and Maguire, *Design and Plan in the Country House,* 2008). Households had shrunk and privacy was becoming increasingly fashionable. So, like many of their peers, the Barnebys divided the Hall horizontally. This new floor separated the family from their servants, and created at least three new bedrooms for John and his eleven children.

The floor remained until 1871, when architect John Buckler removed it to return the Hall to a medieval shape. Today the Gallery is all that remains of the bedroom floor – it was probably designed by Buckler to give the impression of a minstrel's gallery, but was never used for this purpose. Once again, the Hall became a social centre, used for parties and shooting party dinners. Employees' quarters were now at the rear of the house.

'The dining hall remained miraculously preserved, with its vaulted ceiling and uneven rafters; a long narrow table stood in the middle of it; and at the far end branches, heaped in the open hearth, and blazing, partly lit the dim place.'

Constance Sitwell recalls a shooting party at Lower Brockhampton in autumn 1919 in *Smile at Time*, 1942

Left Looking towards the fireplace and Colonel Lutley's gun collection

Bottom The portraits of the former owners of Brockhampton that adorn the walls in the Great Hall. From L-R: Thomas Barneby (1587–1648), Richard Barneby (1644–1719/20), Isabella's husband (see page 21) and John Barneby Esq (1684–1726)

The 20th-century Hall

When the Freegard farming family moved in, in 1952, they used this space for storing equipment. At the time, it was the only room open to the public and visitors recall seeing it filled with sacks of seed and drums of fuel. Marian Freegard once said that her husband would have stored his tractor here if he could!

The guns

Above the fireplace hangs part of Colonel Lutley's gun collection (the rest can be seen at the Worcester Regimental Museum). Perhaps the most unusual artefact is the spring gun. Such weapons were once used to guard property. They would be attached to a tripwire; if a poacher or intruder crossed this, the gun would rear up to shoot them. Perhaps as a result, spring guns were made illegal in 1827; afterwards some groups aimed to destroy those that remained, making Lutley's a rare survival.

The tables

These 17th-century walnut tables are some of the few furnishings original to Brockhampton. In 1765, Bartholomew Barneby took them to his new mansion for use in the servants' quarters. They were returned to Lower Brockhampton when the National Trust took it over in 1946. Today they are set with places for former residents and owners.

The paintings

These portraits were saved from the Barnebys' Georgian mansion. They represent the last five generations of the family to live in the manor house (in clockwise order, starting from the door): Thomas Barneby, his son John, John's son, Richard, Richard's son John and John's nephew, Bartholomew.

John Barneby Esq.re

Isabella Barneby's
Room (1685)

In the spring of 1684, 39-year-old Richard Barneby found himself the new owner of Brockhampton. His father, John, had passed away and as the eldest of 11 children he inherited the estate. By the spring of 1685 he had moved into Lower Brockhampton, bringing with him his pregnant wife, Isabella, and their three children. This room looks as Isabella might have had it at this time.

When Isabella, ten years Richard's junior, married her husband in 1678 she was probably accustomed to a high standard of living. Her father was a Judge and MP for Bewdley, while her mother was the daughter of Sir Edwin Sandys, an MP and entrepreneur. This is perhaps how her family afforded to provide their new son-in-law with a settlement of £1,500 (the equivalent of around £200,000 today) prior to his and Isabella's marriage. Thereafter the couple increased their fortune through money made from rents, the sale of produce from the Brockhampton estate and assets that included a London house and stocks and shares.

Sadly they were not so fortunate when it came to their family, losing three of their seven children early in their lives. Nicholas (born c.1680) and Richard (c.1681) died aged 21 and 19 respectively. Their fourth child, Thomas, died in childhood. (We don't know the cause of their deaths.) Their eldest child Penelope, and her younger siblings, John (who inherited Brockhampton), Edmund and Mary, all survived. However, these survival rates were actually above average for the 17th century, when 60% of children died before their 16th birthday.

The room today

The oak bed, dating from 1645, is currently on loan from Croft Castle. The bedsheet shows Isabella's instructions to her maid for preparing for bed, from brushing out fleas to providing a midnight feast between Isabella's first and second sleeps.

The decorative crewelwork hangings would also have kept out draughts and offered privacy when the maid came to wake her employers. The replica work on display here was made in the 1970s using Indian fabrics. It is by Frances Kaye for Diana Uhlman, then Chatelaine at Croft Castle.

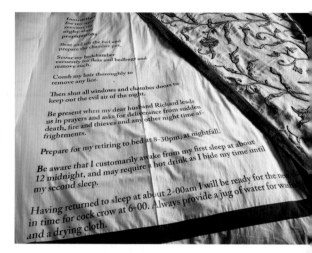

What was once here?

This and the neighbouring bedroom (see page 27) were once the Great Chamber. Guests and family members, usually ladies, would retire here from the activities of the Great Hall. Access would probably have been by an outside staircase as the current, internal one wasn't built until the 1870s. Between 1660 and 1680, Richard's father, John, divided the Great Chamber and the anteroom next to it to create four rooms.

The roof

The roof's remarkable timbers are the residence of colonies of pipistrelle, noctule and brown long-eared bats, which swoop in and out using a custom-made flap. Consequently it is now closed off from the public to protect the species. Special bat-proof covers have been developed to guard the more precious collections from the bats that live elsewhere in the manor house.

Bartholomew Barneby's Room (1750)

When Richard and Isabella's son John died childless in 1726, he left the estate to his nephew, Bartholomew Richard Lutley. Overnight, the 13-year-old boy became a millionaire.

This room looks as Bartholomew might have had it in 1750, almost 25 years after he inherited Brockhampton. By then he had settled in, made a name for himself in the area and had started improving his estate. But his greatest changes were yet to come.

Bartholomew's Brockhampton

Bartholomew didn't take charge of the estate until 1735, after he graduated from Oxford University. This was also when he adopted the name and arms of Barneby, as was required by his uncle's will.

The same year, Bartholomew borrowed the hefty sum of £3,000 from his mother to improve the estate – the equivalent of about £600,000 today. All surviving farms on the estate have buildings that can be dated to Bartholomew's era, including the farmhouse at Warren Farm (see page 46).

But there is also one farm that no longer exists. Hill Farm, which had been worked by Bartholomew's great grandfather, enjoyed views over the Malvern Hills and sometimes even to the Cotswolds beyond. Bartholomew coveted its position. He also found his inherited manor small, dark, old-fashioned and not befitting for a man of his stature in the mid-18th century.

By then, Batholomew had grown increasingly wealthy. In 1756, he married the daughter of family friends, Betty Freeman. She came with a dowry of £3,000 and also inherited money on her father's death in 1764. It's possibly this money that, in 1765, prompted Bartholomew to contact his architect friend Thomas Farnolls Pritchard. Pritchard produced plans for a grand, redbrick mansion, which took Hill Farm's place. It remains today, though is now a private residence.

Once Bartholomew moved to his new home, Lower Brockhampton Manor became a farmhouse. However he still kept it in good condition, and installed a barn for a cow and inserted hooks for hanging hams in the Great Hall's chimney.

A figure of note

Bartholomew quickly became an important local figure. He was made High Sheriff of Herefordshire in 1739, aged 26, and was involved in charitable works such as schemes to raise money for Bromyard's poor. He is commemorated by a memorial in St Peters Church, Bromyard.

Bartholomew's documents

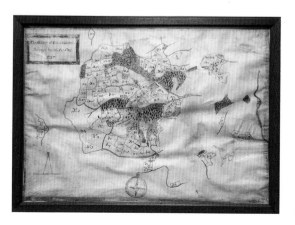

On the table is a transcription of Bartholomew's mother's will. Penelope made generous donations throughout her life, but her accounts were left a mess. After her death in 1745, Bartholomew spent many years trying to unravel her complex affairs.

Hanging on the walls are two documents commissioned by Bartholomew. The parkland design was produced for him in 1769 by Thomas Leggett, but never executed (see page 35). Warren Farm features on the map, so we know it dates to at least this time.

Also on display is a list of Brockhampton's fields and their sizes. This was produced by Inigo Perkins after undertaking an estate survey in 1737, not long after Bartholomew took over management of Brockhampton. The 'A, R and P' in the column headings refer to area measures: A = acre, r = rood (1/4 acre) and p = perch (1/40 of a rood). A corresponding map is also on display on the landing.

Left An oil painting of Bartholomew Barneby né Lutley c.1725–30, artist unknown

Bottom centre The map is a survey of the estate done in 1737 by Jno (John) Perkins on the instructions of Bartholomew Barneby

Top right Costumed volunteer interpreter Martin Attridge dressed as Bartholomew Barneby

Joseph and Ann Curetons' Room (1861)

When the Curetons were living here in 1861, Lower Brockhampton was probably in a poor state of repair. Less than ten years later, Buckler would embark on his massive restoration project. However, Joseph Cureton was an important employee on the estate and it's unlikely he was given completely sub-standard accommodation – so at least some of the seven bedrooms, perhaps including this one, must have been warm and dry.

A local to the area, Joseph had been employed at Brockhampton since at least 1851, when he was an agricultural worker. By 1861 he had been promoted to wagoner, one of the most important positions on the estate. His primary role would have been to look after the estate's horses, arguably the most vital equipment on a Victorian farm. But despite Joseph's senior status, the Curetons were not particularly well off. Most of Joseph's earnings went on food and clothes, reflected in the room's basic furnishings. In 1861, this room may have been used by Joseph, Ann, and three of their seven children – baby John, two-year-old Henry, who shared his parents' bed, and Eliza, aged four, who would have used a truckle bed. Their four elder children (Alice, Mary, George and William) would have shared rooms elsewhere in the house.

A wagoner's life

Joseph's responsibilities would have included looking after the horses' harnesses, repairing vehicles and caring for the horses' health. Each morning, Joseph may have tapped the horses' feet with a knife handle or short stick. If the animal flinched, he would then have checked the shoe and its nails for the cause of the lameness.

Recipes to cure horses' ailments were passed down through generations of wagoners. Treatments included a combination of turpentine, egg yolk and camphor to cure worms; force-feeding a hornet's nest for colic; and a mix of cider vinegar and pickling alum for leg splints.

The room

The Curetons' room is a mix of 15th- and 16th-century features. The upper wall beam dates to 1425 but the lower wall timber dates 100 years later and was put in to support the close-studding that replaced the original build.

This room arguably provides the best example of the Tudor close-studding installed for Richard Habington. Compare the number of timbers in the wall behind the bed with the one around the windows, where there are far more and they're much closer together. The extra material required for the latter would have made this a very expensive design.

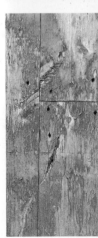

Top right Joseph and Ann Cureton's room, including a cradle and toys that might be similar to ones their children used

Bottom left As a waggoner, it was Joseph Cureton's job to look after the estate's horses

Bottom right A reproduction of a sampler, similar to those made by Alice when practising her needlework skills

Smocks and shoes

This room features a number of items that the Curetons may have worn, including original clogs (though the soles are modern) – pick them up to feel how heavy they are. There is also a replica wagoner's smock, and quilts which sit on the truckle bed were made for Brockhampton by the Newent Quilters.

The sampler is also a reproduction. Samplers were pieces of embroidery, produced – usually by girls – as a demonstration of needlework skills. They tended to include their name and the date the sampler was produced – this one is attributed to Alice, the Curetons' eldest daughter.

Albert Sprague's Room (1915)
The Landing (1871)

Albert Sprague's Room (1915)

On 6 August 1915, 19-year-old Albert Sprague, the only son of Alfred and Sarah, laid out his new kit, ready to check it one final time. But soon, he wouldn't even be in the same country. The next day, he joined the King's Shropshire Light Infantry (KSLI) 6th Battalion as Private 15633, and was sent to the Western Front, to fight in the First World War.

Albert had spent his whole life on the Brockhampton estate: his father was its gamekeeper and, after leaving school, Albert worked there as an agricultural labourer.

Albert never again lived or worked on the estate. He lost his life on 30 November 1917 – by then a Sergeant – when fighting at the Battle of Cambrai. He was one of about 44,000 British men to perish during the offensive, which saw one of the first uses of large tanks in combat, and one of 888,246 military men who lost their lives during the four-year conflict.

Albert has no known grave but is commemorated at the Cambrai Memorial, Louverval.

Bottom left Albert Sprague's room, his army equipment and clothing laid ready for war

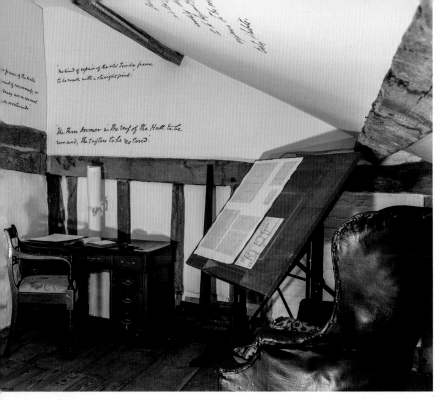

Brockhampton's war

Albert was not the only Brockhampton resident to fight in the First World War. Thirty men on the estate joined up, many to the Worcestershire Yeomanry or Herefordshire Regiment. We're not entirely sure why Alfred chose the KSLI over these more local regiments, though he may have been attracted by the opportunity to go straight to France (the 1st Herefordshire regiment first served in the Gallipoli peninsula and Egypt).

The room

This room came into being when the original anteroom was divided into two under John Barneby in the mid-17th century (see page 21). Original Tudor features include close studding and some fascinating wall pegs. Sited above the bed, these pegs fit perfectly into holes cut for them in the wall. They would have been used to hang clothes, moved in and out of the wall as required. Although there is evidence of these having been included elsewhere in the Manor, these are the only originals left.

The equipment

Replicas of the equipment and uniform Albert took to war are on display, available to be picked up and tried on. Handling the rucksack gives some idea how much weight the young soldiers were expected to bear.

The Landing (1871)

This room is a tribute to the work of John Buckler, who restored the manor in the 1870s (see page 10). He kept a diary of his project, and quotes from this, in his handwriting, can be seen on the wall. A transcript of the whole diary is available to read in this room.

There is also a model timber-framed building, made for Brockhampton by local cabinetmaker Peter Hughes. Visitors can put it together to recreate the historic building process.

A labour of love

On the stairs are paintings of Brockhampton Manor by Bringsty resident William Baron, dating c.1908–1910. A keen amateur photographer and painter, William visited Brockhampton often. During these trips, he fell for the daughter of the estate's gamekeeper William Dennett, and used these paintings to court her. His plan must have been successful as the two married. The five paintings were kindly donated to the National Trust by one of the couple's descendants, Mrs Linda Hendry.

Bottom centre On 15 August 1915, a census recorded information about every man and woman aged between 15 and 65 for a new National Register. One of the key aims was to find out how many men could be spared for war work and join the armed forces

Top centre The landing, with quotes taken from Buckler's diary on the walls

Alice Dennett's Kitchen (1910)

This relatively basic kitchen was the domain of Alice Dennett, the wife of one of Brockhampton's last gamekeepers, William. Here she would have prepared meals and heated water for baths and the weekly clothes wash on Mondays.

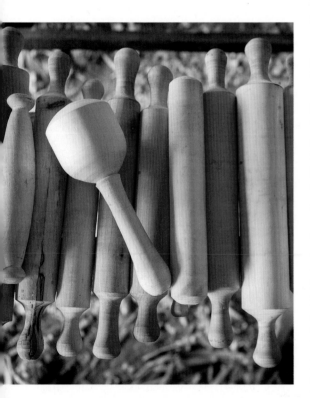

As well as game birds, meals might have included rabbit stew and fruit and vegetables harvested from the estate's fields (turnips and roots in winter and apples, pear and plums in summer). Once a week, Alice would also have baked bread using the purpose-built square oven in the wall, to the right of the stove.

The shooting parties

Held in the autumn and winter, three-day-long shooting parties were one of the highlights of the Edwardian social calendar. Following Buckler's restoration, Lower Brockhampton became a game lodge (as well as tenant farmhouse and gamekeeper's house). Guests staying at the mansion would come down to the Great Hall to dine, catered for by Alice. The local beaters – hired to drive game into the path of the guns – would have dined separately, in Alice's kitchen.

Breakfast, afternoon tea and formal dinners were always served, and sometimes luncheons. By today's standards, breakfasts were very elaborate, containing a selection of meat dishes including game pie and cold beef; curried eggs; herring; and collared eels. Although tea and coffee may have been taken, more popular was a tankard of beer or glass of cherry brandy. We believe Alice prepared their meals with the help of *The Woman's Book: Everything a Woman Ought to Know* (1918), and her copy can be seen in this room.

Left Rolling pins made in the Brockhampton wood-turning shed

Evolution of the kitchen

Lower Brockhampton's first indoor kitchen was built in 1525. This has been modified a number of times over the years: ceilings have been repaired (though three of the beams are still original) and rooms modified until the kitchen reached its present shape. The wall enclosing the larder and the wide chimney for the copper and bread oven were both built in the 19th century, though the oven itself may pre-date this.

Many of the Victorian and Edwardian features are reconditioned and are recent installations but are accurate reflections of the range and units Alice would have used.

The treading hole

In the corner of the room furthest from the stairs is what looks like a trapdoor. This was once a 'treading hole', used for packing dried hops. A bag would have been suspended from the hole and hops from the floor above swept into it. A boy or man would then have stamped on the hops to pack them tightly into the bag. The room directly above is the Landing, so it's possible this was once used as a hop loft (though the hole used has since been hidden by a new floorboard).

Centre A view of the kitchen, a copy of *The Woman's Book* laid out on the table

The Buttery
The Freegards' Lounge (1952)

The Buttery

When it was first built, this was an all-purpose pantry. The floor is slightly below ground level to keep the room – and thus produce – cool. When Richard and Mary Barneby lived here in the 1550s, social gatherings at Lower Brockhampton became more frequent. Consequently more food was needed, and so this room became storage for more specific meals: wet food, hung game and drinks such as cider and beer. It was the butler's responsibility to supply and store food and drink.

The beer and cider barrels on display today are actually imported American whisky barrels. When holes were drilled in them to fit the replica taps, it released the fumes of the whisky – this smell still perfumes this room.

The Malvernian ware jugs and bowls are also more modern than they appear. They were made locally in the 21st century, replicating a style made in the area for at least 300 years since the 13th century.

Bottom The Buttery, including the beer and cider barrels and Malvernian ware jugs on the shelf

The Freegards' Lounge (1952)

Residing here in 1952–89, Valentine (Val), Marian and their four children were the last in a long line of tenant farmers and agricultural workers to live at Lower Brockhampton. By this point, the National Trust had taken over ownership of the estate.

Originally built in the early 15th century as the Domultons' private dining room, this was used by the Freegards as a sitting room. Here their children played and guests were entertained. In the evenings, Val and Marian worked on their accounts and paid their bills at the desk in the corner.

Life on the farm

When the Freegards first moved in, Lower Brockhampton was, in Marian's words, 'quite primitive'. There was no mains electricity, telephone connection or stove – Marian cooked over an open fire in the kitchen, until a renting agent insisted that 'you can't have a farmhouse without a stove', and arranged for an Aga to be installed. Sanitation hadn't really moved on since the earliest days of the Manor, with the privy remaining outdoors and being emptied into the moat, along with rubbish from the farm. Gradually over the next decade, conditions improved, such as the first bathroom being installed in 1954–5.

As tenant farmers, the Freegards looked after 47 hectares (115 acres) of land – almost exactly the same amount that Bernard rented from the Bishop almost 800 years earlier (see page 4). They had a small milking herd of Shorthorn cattle, reared lambs and grew apples and damsons in the established orchards. The family used Val's new Land Rover, a tractor and 'Old George', the last farm horse on the land.

It was not all work however: the Freegard children are said to have had 'adventures', running around the walls of the ruined Norman Chapel (see page 32) and floating across the moat in a tin bath.

A new home in an old house

The room is set up as it may have looked when the Freegards first moved in, featuring books and games from the period. On the desk is a copy of a newspaper from 7 February 1952, announcing the death of King George VI. Other news includes that of British troops in Korea and the possible end of the tea ration later that year, which would leave sugar and sweets as the only rationed food.

The fireplace is not original to the room, but has been restored to how it may have looked in the 1950s.

Top and bottom right
The Freegards' Lounge includes lots of ephemera contemporary with the 1950s, including games and radios

The Chapel

The now-ruined Chapel is one of the longest-standing features of the Brockhampton Estate. During excavations carried out in the summer of 2015, a piece of Malvernian pottery was discovered that dates the Chapel to sometime between 1166 and 1200, during Bernard of Brockhampton's era. But the structure seen today is probably quite different from the one he first built here.

It was instead mostly timber and daub (daub is a mixture of mud and dung, which becomes hard when it sets). We think the only surviving aspect of this first construct is the shallow foundations.

The stone building is likely the work of John Domulton. We know he installed windows in the south, east and north and probably inserted the octagonal font. Then in 2015, archaeological experts suggested that the entire building, with the exception of the foundations, appears to have been built in one go. So far from just enhancing the Chapel as we originally believed, John may well have had a whole new structure built for him. Like the Moat and Gatehouse later, this major upgrade was probably a way for the family to show off their wealth and importance to visitors.

Although much of Domultons' Chapel – constructed using local stone – is now lost, the 2015 excavations tell us that it probably once had stone roof-tiling with ceramic green glazed ridge tops, and walls plastered with a lime whitewash. Fragments of green glazed tiles were also discovered around the moat, which suggests the manor house's original roof may have mirrored the Chapel's.

How was it used?

The earliest record of services and clergy here is 1308; these continued until 1402. During that time its patron was almost always the estate owner, who was responsible for providing financial support and ensuring the building's upkeep. But there is an apparent break in the attendance

Top left The Chapel, seen from across the Moat

Top right View from the south west looking towards the east window, thought to have been installed as part of the Domulton family's additions and renovation of the chapel building

of clergy from 1402 until May 1757. It's possible that during this time the building became a 'chapel-of-ease', a privately owned chapel which hosted periodic services for those who couldn't reach churches in Bromyard. Marriages and baptisms also happened here, though the former could only take place under special license granted from the Bishop. No burials are recorded during this period.

There's no definite record of when the Chapel stopped being used permanently, but this possibly coincided with the construction of the new church at the top of the estate. Bartholomew moved into the mansion before the new church was built. However the Chapel didn't fall into disrepair until much later: John Habington Lutley apparently remembered it being in a usable state in around 1845, but by the time Buckler was here in 1870, it had become 'encumbered with rank weeds and parasitic plants'.

The Wider Estate

There is plenty to discover at Brockhampton beyond the moated Manor: from sculpted parkland to woods that feel untouched by human hands, working farmland to orchards bursting with fruit.

The Parkland

In 1769, not long after Bartholomew Barneby had built his new mansion, Thomas Leggett was commissioned to produce a layout for the parkland, the design for which can be viewed in Bartholomew's room in the manor (see page 22). Leggett's ambitious plans – which included a serpentine lake and extending the grounds by 162 hectares (400 acres) – were never realised, but the Barnebys still sculpted their estate. Bartholomew and his son John planted trees, took out field boundaries and converted arable land, orchards and hop grounds into designed land. By 1829 the parkland comprised about 40 hectares (100 acres), mostly east of Brockhampton House. Carriageways were also cut into sloping parkland around the estate, the tracks of which can still be made out in the hills today.

Bartholomew ornamented his estate with conifers such as redwoods, cedars and pines, which are scattered across the land singly or in small clumps. In spring, these trees are favoured by jays and chaffinches, who feed on their pine cones.

Top A view across the Brockhampton Estate and to the Shropshire hills beyond, including Bartholomew's Georgian mansion (now rented privately)

Thomas Leggett

Although his name is not particularly well-known to us now, Thomas Leggett was part of a second wave of naturalistic landscape designers who emerged around this time as the style increased in popularity, following in the footsteps of those such as the renowned Lancelot 'Capability' Brown. Leggett was also responsible for the ten-mile walk at Attingham Park, Shropshire.

Brockhampton House

Built in 1765, Bartholomew's 53-room redbrick Georgian mansion comes complete with stables, servants' wing and no fewer than seven bathrooms. It was designed by Thomas Farnolls Prichard (c.1723–1777), a Shrewsbury-born architect and interior designer perhaps best known for designing the world's first iron bridge at Coalbrookdale, Shropshire. Pritchard also undertook projects for Bartholomew's two brothers-in-law. With an old-fashioned (for the time) entrance hall and Robert Adam-esque painted swags in the dining room, Brockhampton House is considered typical of Pritchard's work.

The house is thought to have been altered in the 19th century but some original features remain into the 21st century, including wine bins in the basement, oak panelling and staircases, marble chimney pieces, and appropriately themed plasterwork in the music room. Constance Sitwell, who stayed there in 1919, remembered Chippendale bookcases in alcoves, gold rosettes on Georgian wallpaper and a gold-and-white ceiling. It also has a parterre, knot garden, wooded spring garden and walled kitchen garden.

The freehold of the Grade II-listed building belongs to the National Trust but it and its 3.2 hectares (8 acres) of land are now a private residence. It stood empty for many years after coming to the Trust in 1946 but was eventually leased to an insurance company in the 1980s, who used it as an office and restored both house and grounds. Since 1996, the house has been under a 125-year leasehold. Leaseholders are obliged to 'keep the property in good and tenantable repair, decoration and condition', but they also pay a capital fee to the Trust so that we insure the property and carry out any necessary repairs to the building's structure.

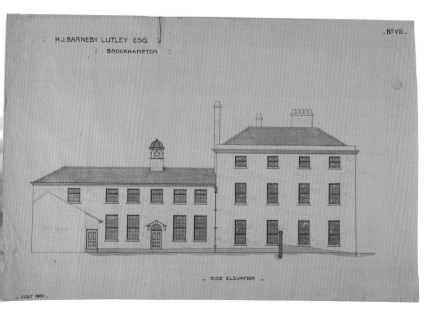

Bottom left and right Plans produced in 1865 for the mansion's formal garden (left) and exterior (right)

The Woodland

Brockhampton's 280 hectares (700 acres) of woodland are hugely varied: at least 32 species of tree, of different ages, have been recorded here.

Ancient trees

Clustered in steep-sided dingles next to the streams, and to the north of the estate, are pockets of semi-natural ancient woodland (ancient woodland refers to an area that has been continuously wooded since at least 1600). These are made up of ash, beech, sycamores and some wide-bottomed oaks known to be at least 500 years old. There are also some limes, and sweet and horse chestnuts.

Plants

If you're walking through the woodland in spring, look out for bluebells, snowdrops, daffodils, primroses and sweet woodruff. Less commonly seen, though still present, are wood spurge and dog's mercury.

Wildlife

Brockhampton's woodlands are a magnet for birds: great and lesser-spotted woodpeckers, pied flycatchers, redstart and great tits can all be seen (or, in the case of the woodpeckers, heard) here. The clearings attract buzzards, sparrowhawks and kestrels as they seek out a meal.

Once trees have died, their fallen, decaying trunks make an ideal home for insects, fungi and lichens.

Although they're unlikely to be spotted by our daytime visitors, the wider estate is also home to a number of bat species, including the soprano pipistrelle, greater and lesser horseshoe and the extremely rare Daubenton's. Badgers and foxes are also known to forage around the woodland floor.

Lawn Pool

Looking up to Bartholomew's mansion, this tranquil triangular pond is one of the woodland's most distinctive features. Our first record of there being water here is in Thomas Leggett's 1769 parkland design (see page 34), when he proposed a serpentine lake in the area. However we're not sure if the current pool is an amendment of his design or whether it was a pre-existing landscape feature that Leggett was proposing to extend. Regardless, it would have been a useful spot for the Barnebys to fish and shoot, and they had a boathouse here in the late 19th century.

Today it is the ideal place to rest your feet during one of our estate walks. See if you can spot carp, frogs and toads splashing in the water, or one of the coots, kingfishers or moorhens.

Top left Come nightfall, foxes are often active in the Brockhampton woodland

Bottom left Beech tree in the ancient woodland to the north of the estate

Centre The peaceful, triangular Lawn Pool

Woodland Produce

The woodland trees are, and always have been, a valuable resource.

In the past, oaks were sold to constructors of wooden houses and warships. Ancient woodlands were also used to make charcoal: circles of blackened earth mark the sites of charcoal burning platforms.

In the 1950s, Norway spruces, larches and Douglas firs were introduced to supply the local markets. More recently, oaks were used to restore Lower Brockhampton Manor after it was damaged by a flood in 2007, and the estate office, visitor reception and Old Apple Store tea room were all constructed from estate timber.

Bottom left Bluebells carpeting the floor indicate that this area is ancient woodland, ie that it has existed since at least 1600

Looking after the woods

A key practice used to look after the woodland is coppicing, a traditional method of woodland management probably as old, if not older, than the woodland itself. Coppicing involves cutting down suitable young tree stems to near ground level; the tree will then regrow without needing to be replanted. When managed correctly, coppicing enables trees to live for hundreds of years. It also allows different light levels through to the woodland floor, which increases biodiversity. The coppiced wood can be turned into environmentally friendly products such as bean poles or sticks and charcoal.

We are also beginning to replace the conifer plantations with native broadleaf trees with the aim of encouraging woodland birds such as pied flycatchers and marsh tits.

Centre top A stack of harvested timber waiting to be collected in Brockhampton's woods

Centre bottom An ancient tree stump now home to many insect species

Bottom right Visitors can enjoy a number of walks taking in Brockhampton's woodland

The Orchards

'Have you ever been here when the blossom is out? … it's heartbreakingly lovely, – the white blossom and the blue blue country stretching away beyond; there are damsons in the hedges, and cherries, and, most beautiful of all, the high old pear trees with their branches curling downwards.'

– Constance Sitwell, *Smile at Time*, 1942

Brockhampton's orchards are hard to miss. Comprising 50 hectares (124 acres), they are some of the largest of any National Trust property. Constance Sitwell may have enjoyed their spring blossom, but come autumn, the gnarly branches of the estate's orchard trees provide an equally attractive but even more practical offer: bountiful apples, cherries, pears and damsons.

The damson

Britain's hedgerows play host to a number of damson varieties. But the type now planted in Brockhampton's orchards, the Shropshire prune, is possibly the oldest, dating from at least the late 1500s (it is named on a tapestry from this period, currently on display at Shrewsbury Museum). It has also been said to be the most flavoursome!

In its heyday, the damson was not just an important food source. It was also used as dye for cotton, wool and leather, including for gloves and carpets. During the First World War, soldiers 'marched off to Gallipoli and the Somme with the khaki of Shropshire damsons on their backs' (Katherine Swift, *The Morville Hours*, 2008) – the fruit was used to produce the colour of their uniforms.

The introduction of artificial dyes has lessened the need for damsons, and so their presence in Britain has decreased. However Herefordshire – and particularly areas around Bromyard – is home to the highest concentration of damson trees in Britain. In September, fruits are found at Brockhampton in abundance – bring a bag to fill and pick your own.

Wildlife

Brockhampton's orchards also provide food and shelter for over 1,000 species, including many types of bats, birds, insects and owls. The rare lesser spotted woodpecker is sometimes heard as it digs for dinner, while bees are attracted to orchard flowers. Butterflies and moths such as the common blue and six-spot burnet flitter on the outskirts, attracted by the bird's foot-trefoil wildflower that grows here.

The orchards are also home to some rare insects, including the noble chafer beetle, whose grubs live in decaying wood. Adults are a striking iridescent bottle green. Other rare types of beetle found in the orchards and wider estate include the *Dorcatoma dresdensis* woodworm beetle, *Scirtidae* marsh beetles and *Buprestidae* jewel beetles. The orchards are also home to the tiny (3mm) mistletoe weevil: Brockhampton was the first place in Britain where this insect was discovered, in 2000, though it has since been found in neighbouring counties.

Orchards: their rise, fall and rise

Orchards have been part of the British landscape since at least the Norman Conquest, and possibly even since the Romans. But since reaching the height of their popularity in the 17th and 18th centuries, their future has been precarious.

The first decline of orchards was halted by the Industrial Revolution. The introduction of cheap sugar and railways increased demand for fresh orchard fruits for jams, and allowed for easier transportation of the product. After the introduction of the railway locally in 1852, Herefordshire apples were sold in markets across the Midlands and London.

But orchards' renewed popularity didn't last forever, and their second decline came sometime after 1950. Many had been turned into vegetable plots in the 1940s, as part of the Second World War's 'Dig for Victory' campaign. Others vanished as towns, cities and infrastructure, such as roads and airports, began to grow. In 1991, many apple orchards were lost under a government scheme aiming to prevent apple overproduction in the European Economic Community. And so between 1950 and the 21st century, almost 60% of Britain's orchards disappeared.

Left A poster advertising the 'Dig for Victory' campaign, which was set up in the Second World War to urge British people to grow food. Across the country, open spaces became allotments, from domestic gardens to public parks, and even the lawn outside the Tower of London

Top left The blossom in Brockhampton's orchard

Bottom left Protecting young apple trees

Top right A remnant orchard at Hill House Farm

Bottom right An illustration of Cowarne apples from Thomas Andrew Knight's *Pomona Herefordiensis*, published in 1811

Restoring the orchards

In recent years, organisations have begun to highlight and act on this worrying decline of British heritage. In 2008 the National Trust launched the Orchard Project in conjunction with a number of other organisations, including Natural England who provided funding from their biodiversity fund. The aim was to 'improve the condition and increase the extent of traditional orchards throughout England'. Brockhampton was one of the 35 National Trust properties targeted, and our current orchards were 'gapped up' with new trees.

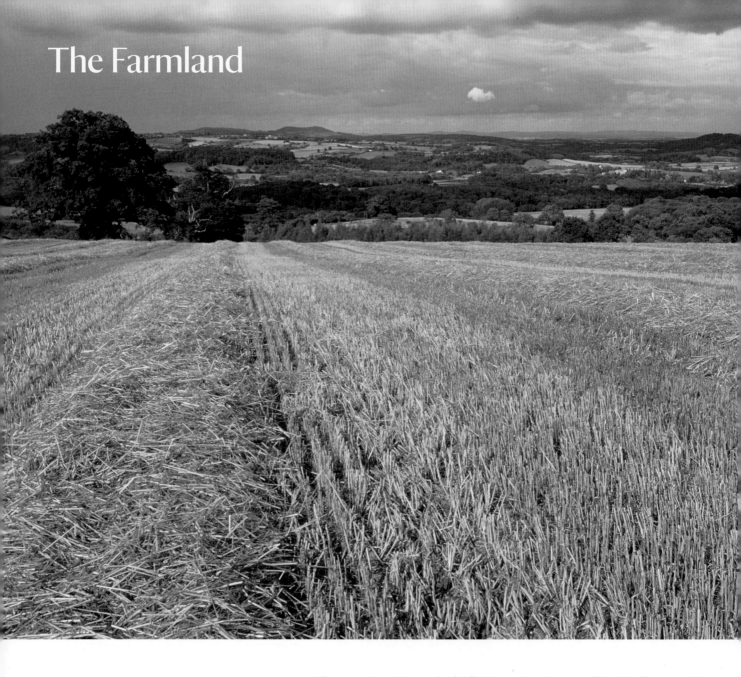

The Farmland

'[Lower Brockhampton's] charm is enhanced by the farmyard activity beside it and the prevailing smell of pigs and manure'
– James Lees-Milne, *People and Places*, 1992

Land use by %	1737	2007
Arable (wheat and barley)	27.7	18.2
Hops	2.4	0
Orchard	2.4	5
Pasture	21.7	47.1
Meadow	6.3	0
Woodland	15.4	24.7
Coppice	7.3	1
Not specified	16.4	4

Left A harvested wheat field

Centre Dinner time for the pedigree Herefordshire cattle at Warren Farm

Above right One of Warren Farm's Ryeland sheep

Martyn Cox is the third generation in his family to work at Lower Norton, one of four farms remaining at Brockhampton. Much has changed on the estate since his grandparents moved here in 1918. Equipment has been mechanised and running water made easily available – Martyn's mother, Margaret, collected water from a stream until she was 16. Boundaries have also changed; Martyn farms 90 hectares (220 acres) of land, compared to the 26 (65 acres) his grandparents looked after. And just under thirty years into the family's tenancy, Brockhampton was bequeathed to the Trust.

But in many ways, this remains a traditional Herefordshire farm. The family grow crops and look after a mixed stock of sheep and cows, the same breeds that were reared here a century ago. Martyn and Sally's children also work on the farm, and pass down these traditions to their own children.

The story is similar elsewhere on the estate, of which just over 400 hectares (1,000 acres) is farmland. Sometimes you might spot Ryeland sheep, a breed that originated in Herefordshire, grazing in the orchards. Hereford cattle have been reared here more or less continuously since 1897. Most of the land is used in the same way as it was almost 300 years ago, with arable land (for growing wheat and barley), pasture and woodland always being the most extensive.

But that's not to say that nothing is changing here.

Farming at Brockhampton today

James and Victoria Hawkins of Warren Farm are responsible for some of Brockhampton's most prominent farmland. They look after the historical herd of Hereford cows on behalf of the National Trust. You might spot them working in the barns next to the shop, or tending sheep in fields next to the manor.

With sons in tow, the Hawkins moved here in 2001, attracted by a shared commitment with the National Trust to look after the land with the long-term landscape in mind. Since moving in, their achievements include introducing wildlife habitats by restoring hedges and conserving damson orchards. They also hope to develop wetland habitats using the farm's natural water course.

The need for change

In 2000, foot and mouth disease devastated the countryside. Almost all of Brockhampton's livestock had to be slaughtered. For the Hawkins, the impact of the disease highlighted the need to diversify, rather than be reliant on livestock. They still raise sheep and cattle for meat – the Hereford breed was reintroduced in 2003 – but also sell products made from other crops on the estate: rapeseed is turned into award-winning rapeseed oil. They also have a vegetable patch, run a bed and breakfast and host educational trips.

A unique proposition

Perhaps the main difference between 'typical' farmers and those who are tenants of the National Trust is the way the public become entwined with their work, with James taking time out of his working day to speak to visitors about what he is doing and answer questions. Visitors also have to be considered when going about day-to-day chores, many of which – such as spraying crops and moving cattle – are planned around Brockhampton's opening hours.

Left Tenant farmers Victoria and James Hawkins, with National Trust advisor (centre) Vicky Bennett, at Warren Farm

Centre A selection of the various products for sale at Warren Farm

Right Award-winning cold pressed rapeseed oil produced at Warren Farm

More to Explore

Gathered your damsons from the orchard and explored every room of Lower Brockhampton Manor? Here are some more of our favourite things to do on the estate.

Go for a walk

Pull on your walking boots and follow one of the waymarked paths. You can choose from shorter, more accessible trails or escape to the wilder, wide estate and enjoy the peace and tranquillity of the woodlands.

Explore the natural play trail

Build a den, play on a giant xylophone and much more. Starting in the orchard next to Lower Brockhampton Manor, the natural play trail takes you on a mile-long journey through Paradise Wood – though you don't have to complete the whole trail before turning back! It's flat and fairly accessible, even for three-wheeled buggies but as it's an unsurfaced, natural path it can get muddy. Keep your eyes peeled for birds of prey, mini beasties and rare woodpeckers as you go.

Stay for longer next time

Brockhampton doesn't have to be just a day visit. There are three holiday cottages on the estate, sleeping between three and ten people. Old Linceter offers a taste of what life might have been like for Bartholomew Barneby, with views across the estate and beyond. Nestled in a valley and surrounded by a stream, the romantic, 15th-century Old Mill Cottage offers a perfectly isolated retreat. Beer enthusiasts will enjoy the 18th-century Oast House, which still has former hop kilns in place. For more information or to book a stay, visit www.nationaltrustholidays.org.uk or phone 0344 335 1287.

Discover old buildings with new purpose

Due to the sheer number and age of the buildings on the estate, inevitably some can no longer be used for their original purpose. However we are developing ways to look after these and bring them back into use. One of these was the Oast House, a vernacular farm building which would once have been used for drying hops during the brewing process. This has now been converted into a microbrewery. Although modern facilities – such as electricity and water – have been installed, we were careful to ensure original features were maintained.

Top View of Brockhampton Estate nestling in the beautiful Herefordshire countryside